UPL**I**FT
GAMES

ONLINE SAFETY FOR YOUNGER FANS

Spending time online is great fun! Here are a few simple rules to help younger fans
stay safe and keep the internet a great place to spend time:
- Never give out your real name – don't use it as your username.
- Never give out any of your personal details.
- Never tell anybody which school you go to or how old you are.
- Never tell anybody your password except a parent or a guardian.
- Be aware that you must be 13 or over to create an account on many sites. Always check the site
policy and ask a parent or guardian for permission before registering.
- Always tell a parent or guardian if something is worrying you.

Stay safe online. Any website addresses listed in this book are correct at the time of going to print.
However, Farshore is not responsible for content hosted by third parties. Please be aware that online content
can be subject to change and websites can contain content that is unsuitable for children.
We advise that all children are supervised when using the internet.

MIX
Paper | Supporting
responsible forestry
FSC™ C007454

This book is produced from independently certified FSC™ paper
to ensure responsible forest management.

For more information visit: www.harpercollins.co.uk/green

INSIDE THE WORLD OF
ADOPT ME!

HARPER
An Imprint of HarperCollinsPublishers

CONTENTS

WELCOME!

Do you love making friends, exploring new places and discovering new pets? Then you're in the right place! Adopt Me is an experience set on **Adoption Island** – a fantastical world filled with the cutest pets to collect! Whether you're hatching eggs, decorating your home or going on adventures with your pet, you're sure to have lots of fun. This Annual is packed with even more games and adventures . . . so let's get started!

My name is: . . . .

I am . . . . years old.

My favorite pet in Adopt Me is: . . . .

Its name is: . . . .

Its favorite trick is: . . . .

My friends in Adopt Me are: . . . .

. . . .

MY NEIGHBORHOOD

There are two main areas in the game: the **Neighborhood** and **Adoption Island**. Players can move between them by walking or driving through the big tunnel.

Every time you log into the game, you'll spawn in your own home in the **Neighborhood**. You can customize your house with decorations and furniture of all shapes, sizes and colors. Once you've been playing for a while, you may be able to upgrade to a bigger house such as a Treehouse, a Castle or a Fairy House.

? If you could live in any house in the **Neighborhood**, what would it look like? Draw it in the space below!

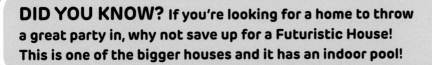

DID YOU KNOW? If you're looking for a home to throw a great party in, why not save up for a Futuristic House! This is one of the bigger houses and it has an indoor pool!

Turn the page to go through the tunnel and learn about **Adoption Island...**

ADOPTION ISLAND

There's so much to see on Adoption Island! Here, you can visit many exciting shops and buildings.

Circle the correct answer to each question! The answers are on page 68.

1 Where do you go to adopt pets?

THE NURSERY

THE BABY SHOP

2 Where do you take your pet when they feel sick?

THE PET SHOP

THE HOSPITAL

3 Where should you take your pet if they're bored?

THE CAR DEALERSHIP

THE PLAYGROUND

4 Where can you find this tasty treat?

THE CAMPSITE

THE PIZZA SHOP

Now Hiring!

5 Where do you go to merge four of the same pet into a Neon Pet?

THE SKY CASTLE

THE NEON CAVE

My favorite place to go on **Adoption Island** is: . . . .

MEET THE DEVELOPERS

In 2017, developers Bethink and NewFissy decided to develop and launch a new game called Adopt Me! The mission was to create a vibrant space for community members to roleplay and explore a magical world where every day is a new adventure.

Adopt Me is now worked on by a team of over 50 amazing people and **Adoption Island** has now been visited over 33 billion times. WOW! Here are some of the incredible members of the team . . .

Hi, I'm **Bethink**, the Creative Director and Co-CEO of Uplift Games. I designed the original Adopt Me universe in 2017 and am now responsible for overseeing the design of the ever-changing landscape of Adoption Island including seasonal updates, locations, pets and objects within it.

WHAT IS YOUR FAVORITE THING ABOUT ADOPT ME?
My favorite thing about Adopt Me is how much it changes – it is a living, breathing world! Shops are always being upgraded and pets are always being added. Right now, I'm working on the small things in Adopt Me, like how to improve the game by weekly updates.

WHAT IS YOUR FAVORITE PET?
The Silly Duck! The pet contains so much character, and the team did an amazing job bringing it to life. If you see me in-game, I almost always have one of them by my side.

Hi, I'm **NewFissy**! At Uplift Games, I have the joy of being a founder of the studio and Co-CEO. My job is quite special within our studio, as I focus on doing all of the essential work that isn't already being done by someone else. In the past three years, I've served as engineer, producer, UI designer, data scientist and many more roles!

WHAT IS YOUR FAVORITE THING ABOUT ADOPT ME?
My favorite thing about Adopt Me is the fans. Seeing players engage with the world we've created brings our team immense joy and inspires us to make Adopt Me the best game possible.

WHAT IS YOUR FAVORITE PET?
My favorite pet is the Frost Fury from the 2020 Winter Holidays event. It's a majestic long blue dragon that exudes a sense of dignity. Its elegant features and magnificent colors always capture the attention and admiration of both its owners and fellow players, and I think our artists did an outstanding job bringing it to life.

Jesse here! I run the team that looks after all our social media and makes the videos you see every week!

WHAT IS YOUR FAVORITE THING ABOUT ADOPT ME?
Reading all the wonderful comments every day makes it so much fun to do this job!

WHAT IS YOUR FAVORITE PET?
My very own pop idol Glyptodon, named Barv!

Hi, I'm **ColoredCookies**. I'm one of two 2D Artists! I dabble in a little bit of everything: the buttons you press in-game, the coloring pages you doodle on, and much more!

WHAT IS YOUR FAVORITE THING ABOUT ADOPT ME?
My favorite thing has to be the people, which includes not only my colleagues, but also the Adopt Me community! It takes the right amount of kindness, patience and memes to cultivate environments that are so supportive and endearing.

WHAT IS YOUR FAVORITE PET?
The Goldhorn! One of my first releases was the Mythic Egg, and I absolutely fell in love with the Goldhorn's design. It radiates both elegance and cuteness!

Hi, I'm **EgoMoose**! I'm a Staff Gameplay Engineer. I get to write the code that powers new and exciting features for Adopt Me!

WHAT IS YOUR FAVORITE THING ABOUT ADOPT ME?
I love seeing what players create. One of my favorite things is to look at YouTube channels where people make interesting builds that I didn't think were possible.

WHAT IS YOUR FAVORITE PET?
My go-to is my Cerberus (the three-headed dog) named Hee Haw. I styled it to look like a cowboy, and in my head the different heads take turns wearing the hat.

PET ADVENTURES, PART 1

It was a bright and sunny day on Adoption Island. The pets were all gathered outside the Nursery when the Unicorn arrived, with a very exciting message:

Guess what? There's going to be a big party on Adoption Island!

Wow! I love parties! Where is it?

That's the mystery! To find out where the party is, we have to visit five places on Adoption Island first, and solve a puzzle at each one. Each puzzle will give us a piece of the secret invitation!

That sounds like a treasure hunt!

It *is* a treasure hunt!

Then let's get started! Where do we go first?

To take part in this treasure hunt,
First find a special shop,
Where warm and tasty food is served
With red sauce on the top!

I know where we should start . . .

? Where do you think the Unicorn and the Red Panda should go?
Circle the place, and then turn the page to see if you're correct!

PLAYGROUND

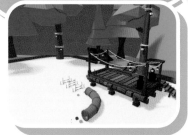

PIZZA SHOP

PET SHOP

The Unicorn and the Red Panda arrived at the ... PIZZA SHOP! The first part of the secret party invitation was waiting for them in the form of a word search puzzle.

PUZZLE #1

Can you help the Unicorn and the Red Panda by finding these pizza toppings hidden in the word search?

- ☐ Cheese
- ☐ Peppers
- ☐ Pepperoni
- ☐ Tomatoes
- ☐ Sausage
- ☐ Mushrooms
- ☐ Onions
- ☐ Basil

P	L	D	E	A	R	F	R	I	T
E	I	E	N	E	D	S	P	S	O
P	S	A	U	S	A	G	E	N	M
P	A	T	H	E	E	F	P	O	A
E	B	I	R	E	S	T	P	I	T
R	W	O	R	H	D	Y	E	N	O
O	O	U	N	C	E	E	R	O	E
N	D	I	S	H	E	A	S	D	S
I	S	M	O	O	R	H	S	U	M

Answers on page 68

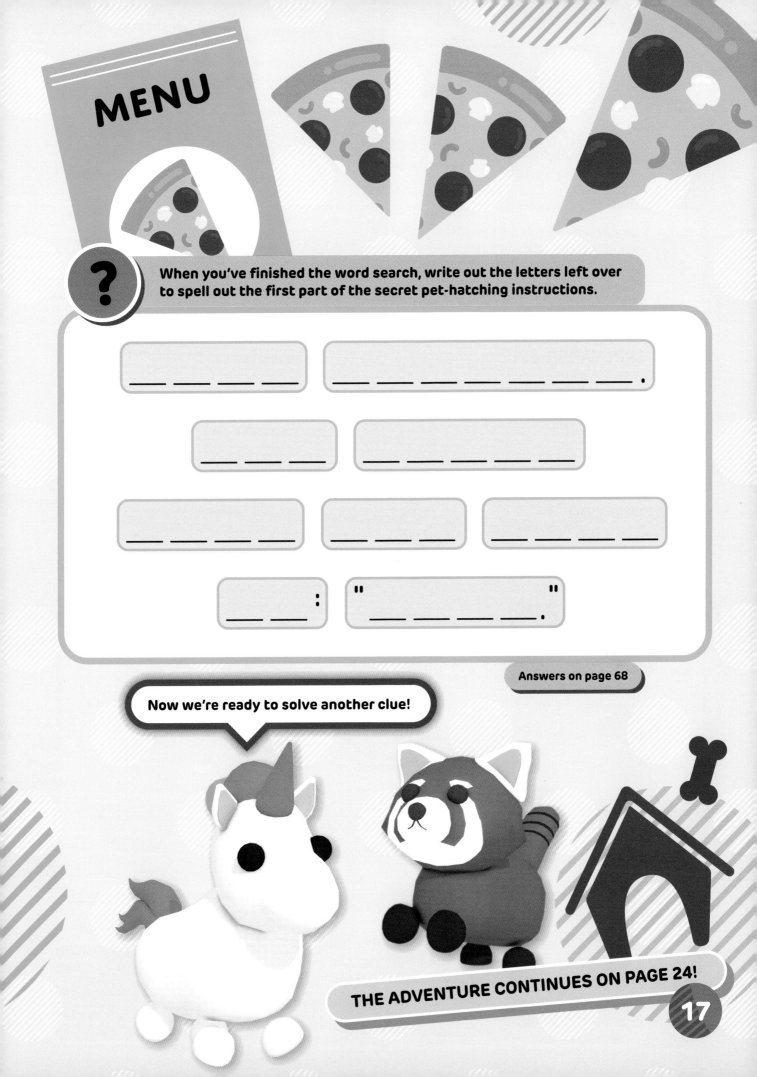

MENU

? When you've finished the word search, write out the letters left over to spell out the first part of the secret pet-hatching instructions.

_____ _____ _____ _____ _____   _____ _____ _____ _____ _____ _____ _____ _____ _____ _____ .

_____ _____ _____ _____   _____ _____ _____ _____ _____ _____ _____

_____ _____ _____ _____ _____ _____   _____ _____ _____ _____   _____ _____ _____ _____ _____

_____ _____ _____ :   " _____ _____ _____ _____ _____ _____ . "

Answers on page 68

Now we're ready to solve another clue!

THE ADVENTURE CONTINUES ON PAGE 24!

FEEDING FUN!

There are lots of foods you can feed your pet when they're hungry – or eat yourself! Can you unscramble these eight tasty treats, and then find them in the grid below?

1 CEI MERCA NECO

....

2 ONCORPP

....

3 SPREYARBR EPI

....

4 LEMONTREAW

....

5 SCHEEE

....

6 THO DGO

....

7 ZIPAZ

....

Answers on page 68

TOP TIP: You don't always have to buy food – there are free donuts at the Salon, you can make your own pizza at the Pizza Shop, free marshmallows at the Campsite and free sandwiches just for logging in!

18

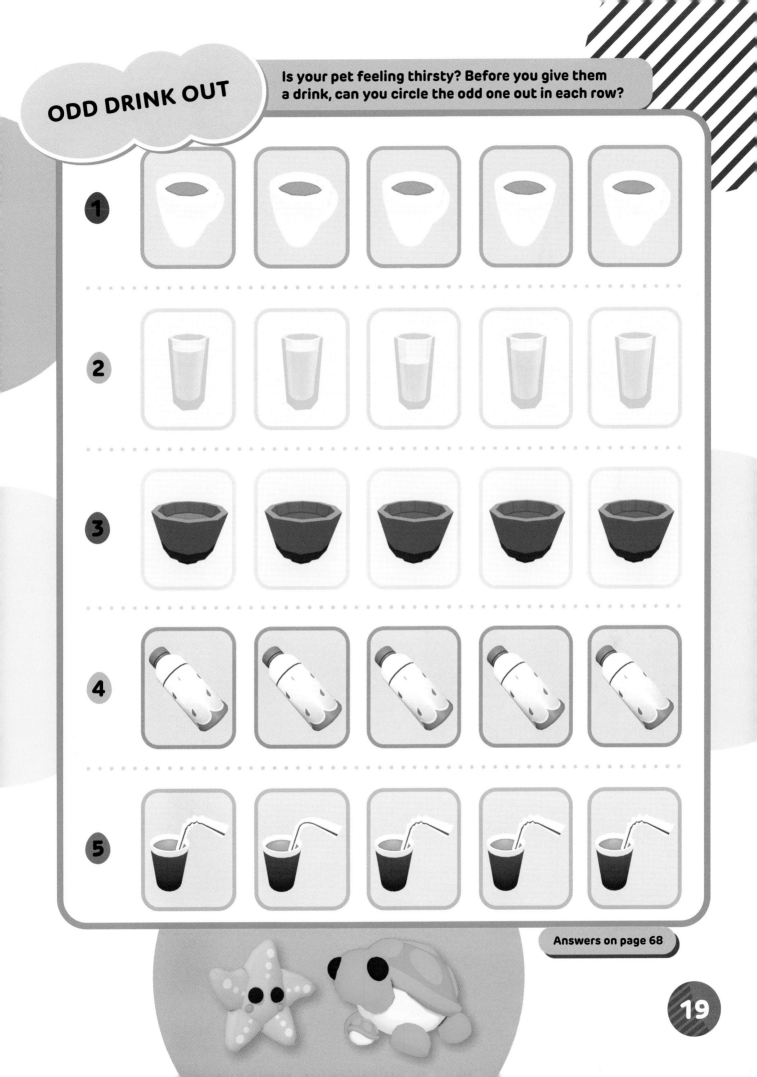

ODD DRINK OUT

Is your pet feeling thirsty? Before you give them a drink, can you circle the odd one out in each row?

Answers on page 68

19

ROOM TO GROW

These two rooms may look the same, but there are five differences in picture 2. Can you spot them all? Color in a heart each time you spot a difference.

picture 1

picture 2

Answers on page 68

Decorating your home can be so much fun! And then you can sit back and relax with your friends and favorite pets! Here are some of our top tips:

YOU DON'T HAVE TO DO IT ALL AT ONCE!

You can change the walls and floors ... add sofas, tables, lamps and beds ... It might seem a bit intimidating, so remember that you don't have to do it all at once! Maybe you want to begin with one room at a time, like the living room ... or maybe you just want to start with a piece of furniture that looks so cute!

CHOOSE YOUR FAVORITE COLORS

Do you want blue walls? Pink walls? Rainbow walls? The choice is yours! Whenever it's an option, it helps to try out a few different colors to see which works best in your home. You can always change it later!

BE AS CREATIVE AS YOU LIKE

Did you know that you can place up to 3,900 furniture items in a single house? Wow! If you're not sure where to start, why not choose a theme ... and then let your imagination run wild!

EVENT SPOTLIGHT:
APRIL FOOL'S DAY

Dashing through the snow, it's . . . wait a minute! Snow in the springtime? Thanks to a prank from Burt, this Christmas-like Egg was around to honor April Fool's Day!

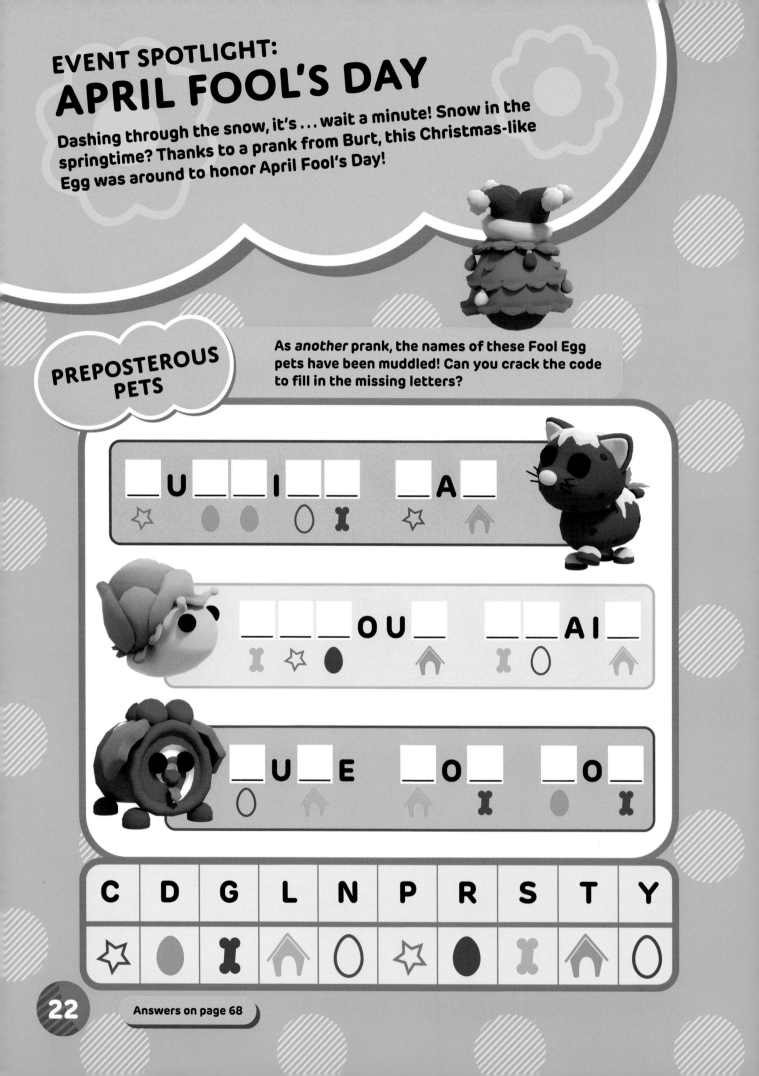

PREPOSTEROUS PETS

As *another* prank, the names of these Fool Egg pets have been muddled! Can you crack the code to fill in the missing letters?

__ U __ __ I __ __ __ A __

__ __ __ __ O U __ __ __ A I __

__ U __ E __ __ O __ __ __ O __

C	D	G	L	N	P	R	S	T	Y

WEIRD AND WONDERFUL PETS

Now it's your turn to come up with new ideas for pets – the weirder, the better! Ask a friend or a family member to answer these eight questions below. Now you can use their answers to create your new pets!

Would you rather have a pet that can fly or swim? . . . .

Would you rather have a pet that has six eyes or three tails? . . . .

Now create a new pet based on their answers!

Would you rather have a pet that is smooth or prickly? . . . .

Would you rather play with your pet on the beach or in the snow? . . . .

Now create a new pet based on their answers!

Would you rather have a pet that sleeps in a tree or sleeps underground? . . . .

Would you rather have a pet that glows in the dark or turns pink when it sneezes? . . . .

Now create a new pet based on their answers!

Would you rather have a Christmas-themed pet or a Halloween-themed pet? . . . .

Would you rather have a pet that is spotted or striped? . . . .

Now create a new pet based on their answers!

23

PET ADVENTURES, PART 2

The Unicorn and the Red Panda were very excited as they left the Pizza Shop. But they still had to visit four more places on **Adoption Island** before they could work out how to get to the special party.

I think we should rrrmmfff frrrrgg munch munch.

I beg your pardon?

Sorry, I was finishing my Pepperoni-Cheese Pizza. I said: Let's work out where to go next!

Careful! Don't spill any of that tomato sauce . . .

Oops, too late!

Noooo! OK, don't panic . . . we'll just have to hope the sauce isn't too messy . . .

It's time to find another clue!

It's hidden on your way.

Inside a pink and chilly shop,

Where penguins love to play!

Don't worry! I think I've figured it out...

Me too... and this time please be careful not to spill more food on the clues!

? Where should the Unicorn and the Red Panda head now? Circle the place, and then turn the page to see if you're correct!

ICE CREAM SHOP

COFFEE SHOP

HOT DOG STAND

The Unicorn and the Red Panda arrived at the ICE CREAM SHOP, where they were almost knocked over by King Penguin! Luckily they caught their balance just in time to notice a big sign that had PUZZLE #2 written on it.

Can you help the Unicorn and the Red Panda solve the second puzzle?

	1	2	3	4
A	Raspberry	Mint	Blueberry	Orange
B	Chocolate	Vanilla	Cherry	Grape

I would like the ice cream from 4A!

My favorite flavor is in 2B!

Could I have 1A? Thank you!

PUZZLE #2

Can you figure out which scoop of ice cream everyone wants?

Puffin's ice cream:	. . . .
Polar Bear's ice cream:	. . . .
Arctic Reindeer's ice cream:	. . . .

? Now circle the first letter of each flavor to spell out the second secret word!

☐ ☐ **E** ☐

Answers on page 68

That's two pieces of the secret message! I wonder where we will go next?

THE ADVENTURE CONTINUES ON PAGE 40!

PREPOSTEROUS PETS

Before the Unicorn and the Red Panda could go on to the next clue, they bumped into some of their friends.

You'll never believe what just happened – the Red Panda accidentally spilled tomato sauce all over our treasure hunt clues!

I once fell into the Hot Springs while trying to do my new dancing trick!

One time, I said that I was a Noodle not a Poodle!

And just wait until you hear about the silliest thing that I did . . .

? What does Silly Duck have to say? You decide!

....

....

....

....

....

....

SILLY DUCK'S SILLY QUESTIONS

Silly Duck has some more silly questions for you ...

? What is the silliest thing you could take a bath in?

....

....

? If an Ant pet was best friends with a Tyrannosaurus Rex pet, what would they do together?

....

....

? If you lived inside a giant sandcastle, what games would you play?

....

....

? If you were going to design a new silly shop on Adoption Island, what would it sell?

....

....

? What would you do if you had eight arms?

....

....

Eight arms, just like me!

Now draw a picture of your silly shop. You can color it in with any colors you like!

CAR, PLANE OR TRAIN?

Do you want to get around the island quickly? Fortunately there are many types of vehicles to choose from! Can you work out which close-up picture matches which vehicle?

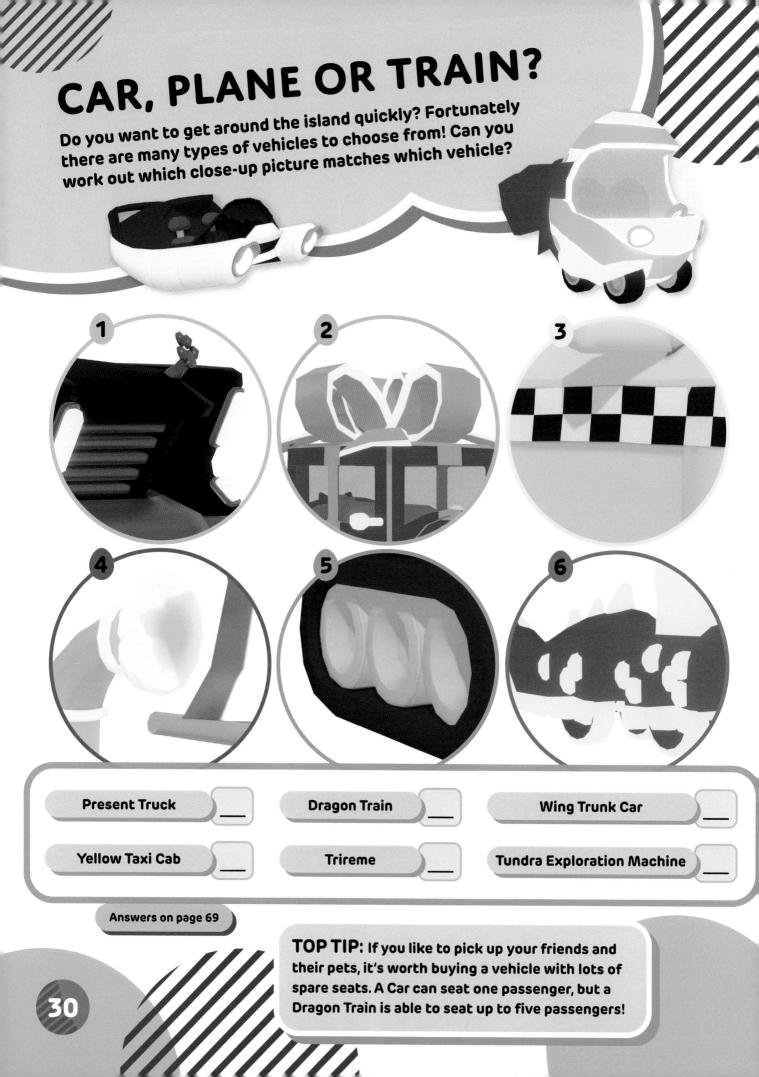

1

2

3

4

5

6

| Present Truck | ___ | Dragon Train | ___ | Wing Trunk Car | ___ |

| Yellow Taxi Cab | ___ | Trireme | ___ | Tundra Exploration Machine | ___ |

Answers on page 69

TOP TIP: If you like to pick up your friends and their pets, it's worth buying a vehicle with lots of spare seats. A Car can seat one passenger, but a Dragon Train is able to seat up to five passengers!

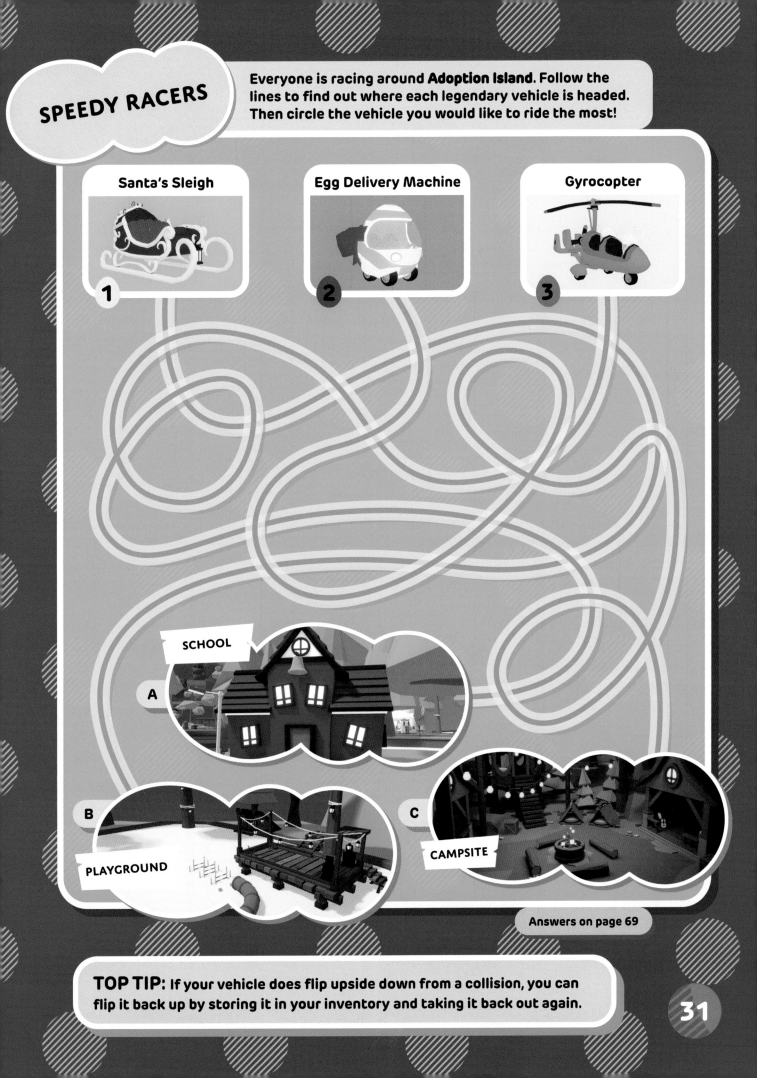

SPEEDY RACERS

Everyone is racing around **Adoption Island**. Follow the lines to find out where each legendary vehicle is headed. Then circle the vehicle you would like to ride the most!

Santa's Sleigh

1

Egg Delivery Machine

2

Gyrocopter

3

SCHOOL

A

B

PLAYGROUND

C

CAMPSITE

Answers on page 69

TOP TIP: If your vehicle does flip upside down from a collision, you can flip it back up by storing it in your inventory and taking it back out again.

PET DIRECTORY ✴ A-Z ✴

There are many pets that can be hatched in Adopt Me and new pets are added all the time! Which ones would you love to adopt? Add a check mark when you have collected each pet!

Alicorn
HATCHES FROM:
Pet, Cracked or Royal Egg
WANT ◯
GOT ◯
LEGENDARY

Ancient Dragon
HATCHES FROM:
Pet, Cracked or Royal Egg
WANT ◯
GOT ◯
LEGENDARY

Angler Fish
HATCHES FROM:
Danger Egg
WANT ◯
GOT ◯
UNCOMMON

Arctic Fox
HATCHES FROM:
Christmas Egg
WANT ◯
GOT ◯
ULTRA-RARE

Arctic Reindeer
HATCHES FROM:
Christmas Egg
WANT ◯
GOT ◯
LEGENDARY

Australian Kelpie
HATCHES FROM:
Aussie Egg
WANT ◯
GOT ◯
RARE

Baku
HATCHES FROM:
Japan Egg
WANT ◯
GOT ◯
LEGENDARY

Bandicoot
HATCHES FROM:
Aussie Egg
WANT ◯
GOT ◯
COMMON

Beaver
HATCHES FROM:
Retired Egg
WANT ◯
GOT ◯
RARE

Black Macaque
HATCHES FROM:
Southeast Asia Egg
WANT ◯
GOT ◯
ULTRA-RARE

Black Panther
HATCHES FROM:
Jungle Egg
WANT ◯
GOT ◯
UNCOMMON

Blue Dog
HATCHES FROM:
Blue Egg
WANT ◯
GOT ◯
UNCOMMON

Brown Bear
HATCHES FROM:
Jungle Egg
WANT
GOT
RARE

Buffalo
HATCHES FROM:
Retired Egg
WANT
GOT
COMMON

Bullfrog
HATCHES FROM:
Woodland Egg
WANT
GOT
COMMON

Bunny
HATCHES FROM:
Retired Egg
WANT
GOT
RARE

Camel
HATCHES FROM:
Pet, Cracked or Royal Egg
WANT
GOT
UNCOMMON

Capybara
HATCHES FROM:
Jungle Egg
WANT
GOT
UNCOMMON

Cat
HATCHES FROM:
Starter or Retired Egg
WANT
GOT
COMMON

Chick
HATCHES FROM:
Easter Egg
WANT
GOT
COMMON

Chocolate Labrador
HATCHES FROM:
Retired Egg
WANT
GOT
UNCOMMON

Clownfish
HATCHES FROM:
Ocean Egg
WANT
GOT
ULTRA-RARE

Cockroach
HATCHES FROM:
Urban Egg
WANT
GOT
COMMON

Corgi
HATCHES FROM:
Pet, Cracked or Royal Egg
WANT
GOT
ULTRA-RARE

Cow
HATCHES FROM:
Farm Egg
WANT
GOT
RARE

Crab
HATCHES FROM:
Ocean Egg
WANT
GOT
UNCOMMON

Crocodile
HATCHES FROM:
Jungle Egg
WANT
GOT
ULTRA-RARE

Crow
HATCHES FROM:
Farm Egg
WANT
GOT
LEGENDARY

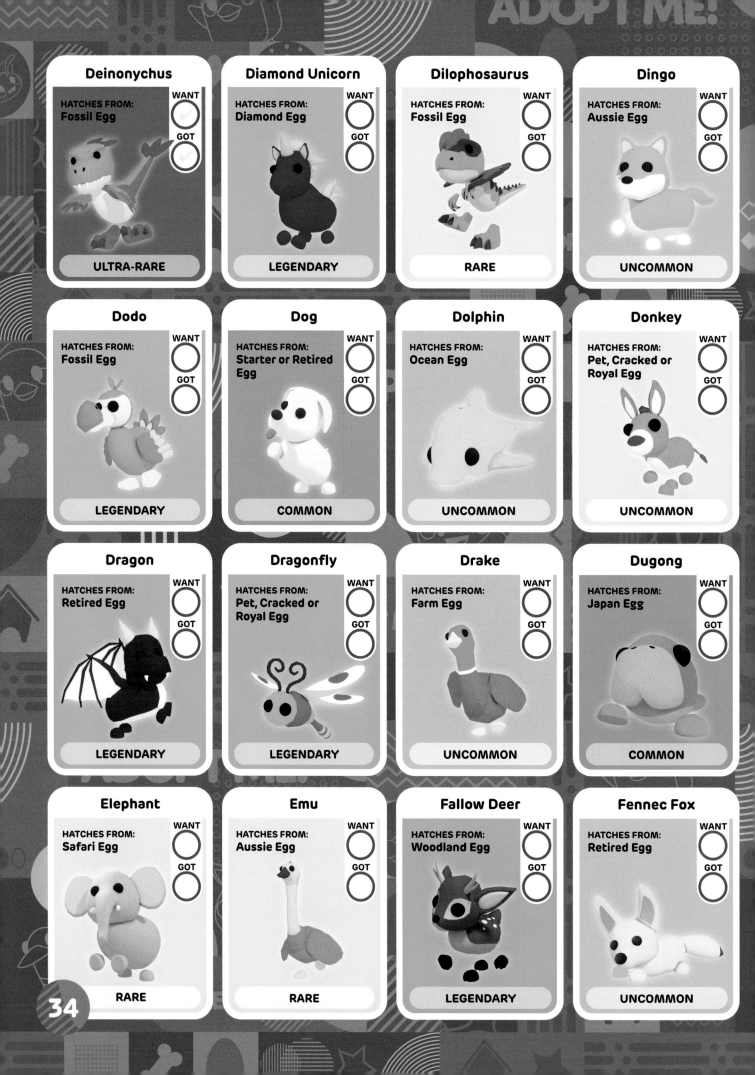

Deinonychus
HATCHES FROM:
Fossil Egg
WANT
GOT
ULTRA-RARE

Diamond Unicorn
HATCHES FROM:
Diamond Egg
WANT
GOT
LEGENDARY

Dilophosaurus
HATCHES FROM:
Fossil Egg
WANT
GOT
RARE

Dingo
HATCHES FROM:
Aussie Egg
WANT
GOT
UNCOMMON

Dodo
HATCHES FROM:
Fossil Egg
WANT
GOT
LEGENDARY

Dog
HATCHES FROM:
Starter or Retired Egg
WANT
GOT
COMMON

Dolphin
HATCHES FROM:
Ocean Egg
WANT
GOT
UNCOMMON

Donkey
HATCHES FROM:
Pet, Cracked or Royal Egg
WANT
GOT
UNCOMMON

Dragon
HATCHES FROM:
Retired Egg
WANT
GOT
LEGENDARY

Dragonfly
HATCHES FROM:
Pet, Cracked or Royal Egg
WANT
GOT
LEGENDARY

Drake
HATCHES FROM:
Farm Egg
WANT
GOT
UNCOMMON

Dugong
HATCHES FROM:
Japan Egg
WANT
GOT
COMMON

Elephant
HATCHES FROM:
Safari Egg
WANT
GOT
RARE

Emu
HATCHES FROM:
Aussie Egg
WANT
GOT
RARE

Fallow Deer
HATCHES FROM:
Woodland Egg
WANT
GOT
LEGENDARY

Fennec Fox
HATCHES FROM:
Retired Egg
WANT
GOT
UNCOMMON

Flamingo

HATCHES FROM:
Safari Egg

WANT ○
GOT ○

ULTRA-RARE

Frog

HATCHES FROM:
Aussie Egg

WANT ○
GOT ○

ULTRA-RARE

Gargoyle

HATCHES FROM:
Urban Egg

WANT ○
GOT ○

LEGENDARY

Gecko

HATCHES FROM:
Southeast Asia Egg

WANT ○
GOT ○

RARE

Glyptodon

HATCHES FROM:
Fossil Egg

WANT ○
GOT ○

UNCOMMON

Goat

HATCHES FROM:
Urban Egg

WANT ○
GOT ○

RARE

Golden Dragon

HATCHES FROM:
Golden Egg

WANT ○
GOT ○

LEGENDARY

Golden Griffin

HATCHES FROM:
Golden Egg

WANT ○
GOT ○

LEGENDARY

Golden Unicorn

HATCHES FROM:
Golden Egg

WANT ○
GOT ○

LEGENDARY

Goldhorn

HATCHES FROM:
Mythic Egg

WANT ○
GOT ○

LEGENDARY

Ground Sloth

HATCHES FROM:
Fossil Egg

WANT ○
GOT ○

COMMON

Hawk

HATCHES FROM:
Woodland Egg

WANT ○
GOT ○

LEGENDARY

Hydra

HATCHES FROM:
Mythic Egg

WANT ○
GOT ○

ULTRA-RARE

Hyena

HATCHES FROM:
Safari Egg

WANT ○
GOT ○

RARE

Ibis

HATCHES FROM:
Japan Egg

WANT ○
GOT ○

RARE

Kangaroo

HATCHES FROM:
Aussie Egg

WANT ○
GOT ○

LEGENDARY

Kirin
HATCHES FROM:
Mythic Egg
WANT ○
GOT ○
UNCOMMON

Koala
HATCHES FROM:
Aussie Egg
WANT ○
GOT ○
ULTRA-RARE

Koi Carp
HATCHES FROM:
Japan Egg
WANT ○
GOT ○
RARE

Leopard Cat
HATCHES FROM:
Japan Egg
WANT ○
GOT ○
RARE

Lion
HATCHES FROM:
Safari Egg
WANT ○
GOT ○
ULTRA-RARE

Llama
HATCHES FROM:
Farm Egg
WANT ○
GOT ○
ULTRA-RARE

Malay Tapir
HATCHES FROM:
Southeast Asia Egg
WANT ○
GOT ○
COMMON

Maneki-Neko
HATCHES FROM:
Japan Egg
WANT ○
GOT ○
LEGENDARY

Meerkat
HATCHES FROM:
Safari Egg
WANT ○
GOT ○
UNCOMMON

Merhorse
HATCHES FROM:
Mythic Egg
WANT ○
GOT ○
RARE

Narwhal
HATCHES FROM:
Ocean Egg
WANT ○
GOT ○
RARE

Octopus
HATCHES FROM:
Ocean Egg
WANT ○
GOT ○
LEGENDARY

Orangutan
HATCHES FROM:
Pet, Cracked or Royal Egg
WANT ○
GOT ○
RARE

Owl
HATCHES FROM:
Farm Egg
WANT ○
GOT ○
LEGENDARY

Parakeet
HATCHES FROM:
Pet, Cracked or Royal Egg
WANT ○
GOT ○
RARE

Parrot
HATCHES FROM:
Jungle Egg
WANT ○
GOT ○
LEGENDARY

Pig
HATCHES FROM:
Farm Egg

WANT ◯
GOT ◯

RARE

Pine Marten
HATCHES FROM:
Woodland Egg

WANT ◯
GOT ◯

ULTRA-RARE

Pink Cat
HATCHES FROM:
Pink Egg

WANT ◯
GOT ◯

UNCOMMON

Phoenix
HATCHES FROM:
Mythic Egg

WANT ◯
GOT ◯

LEGENDARY

Platypus
HATCHES FROM:
Jungle Egg

WANT ◯
GOT ◯

ULTRA-RARE

Polar Bear
HATCHES FROM:
Christmas Egg

WANT ◯
GOT ◯

RARE

Poodle
HATCHES FROM:
Pet, Cracked or
Royal Egg

WANT ◯
GOT ◯

UNCOMMON

Pterodactyl
HATCHES FROM:
Fossil Egg

WANT ◯
GOT ◯

RARE

Puffer Fish
HATCHES FROM:
Danger Egg

WANT ◯
GOT ◯

ULTRA-RARE

Rabbit
HATCHES FROM:
Retired Egg

WANT ◯
GOT ◯

RARE

Red Cardinal
HATCHES FROM:
Woodland Egg

WANT ◯
GOT ◯

UNCOMMON

Red Crowned Crane
HATCHES FROM:
Japan Egg

WANT ◯
GOT ◯

ULTRA-RARE

Red Fox
HATCHES FROM:
Woodland Egg

WANT ◯
GOT ◯

RARE

Red Panda
HATCHES FROM:
Retired Egg

WANT ◯
GOT ◯

ULTRA-RARE

Rhino
HATCHES FROM:
Jungle Egg

WANT ◯
GOT ◯

RARE

Rhino Beetle
HATCHES FROM:
Japan Egg

WANT ◯
GOT ◯

UNCOMMON

Robin
HATCHES FROM:
Christmas Egg
WANT
GOT
COMMON

Robot
HATCHES FROM:
Pet, Cracked or Royal Egg
WANT
GOT
ULTRA-RARE

Sabertooth
HATCHES FROM:
Fossil Egg
WANT
GOT
ULTRA-RARE

Sado Mole
HATCHES FROM:
Japan Egg
WANT
GOT
COMMON

Salamander
HATCHES FROM:
Woodland Egg
WANT
GOT
ULTRA-RARE

Sasquatch
HATCHES FROM:
Mythic Egg
WANT
GOT
RARE

Seahorse
HATCHES FROM:
Ocean Egg
WANT
GOT
RARE

Shark
HATCHES FROM:
Ocean Egg
WANT
GOT
LEGENDARY

Shiba Inu
HATCHES FROM:
Retired Egg
WANT
GOT
ULTRA-RARE

Silly Duck
HATCHES FROM:
Farm Egg
WANT
GOT
UNCOMMON

Snow Cat
HATCHES FROM:
Retired Egg
WANT
GOT
UNCOMMON

Snow Puma
HATCHES FROM:
Retired Egg
WANT
GOT
RARE

Spider Crab
HATCHES FROM:
Japan Egg
WANT
GOT
ULTRA-RARE

Spinosaurus
HATCHES FROM:
Danger Egg
WANT
GOT
LEGENDARY

Stegosaurus
HATCHES FROM:
Fossil Egg
WANT
GOT
UNCOMMON

Stingray
HATCHES FROM:
Ocean Egg
WANT
GOT
COMMON

Swan
HATCHES FROM:
Christmas Egg
WANT
GOT
RARE

Swordfish
HATCHES FROM:
Pet, Cracked or Royal Egg
WANT
GOT
ULTRA-RARE

Tanuki
HATCHES FROM:
Japan Egg
WANT
GOT
UNCOMMON

Tasmanian Tiger
HATCHES FROM:
Fossil Egg
WANT
GOT
COMMON

Trapdoor Snail
HATCHES FROM:
Japan Egg
WANT
GOT
ULTRA-RARE

Triceratops
HATCHES FROM:
Fossil Egg
WANT
GOT
UNCOMMON

Turkey
HATCHES FROM:
Farm Egg
WANT
GOT
ULTRA-RARE

T-Rex
HATCHES FROM:
Fossil Egg
WANT
GOT
LEGENDARY

Unicorn
HATCHES FROM:
Retired Egg
WANT
GOT
LEGENDARY

Wild Boar
HATCHES FROM:
Safari Egg
WANT
GOT
UNCOMMON

Wolf
HATCHES FROM:
Christmas Egg
WANT
GOT
UNCOMMON

Wolpertinger
HATCHES FROM:
Mythic Egg
WANT
GOT
COMMON

Woodpecker
HATCHES FROM:
Woodland Egg
WANT
GOT
RARE

Woolly Mammoth
HATCHES FROM:
Fossil Egg
WANT
GOT
RARE

Wyvern
HATCHES FROM:
Mythic Egg
WANT
GOT
ULTRA-RARE

Zebra
HATCHES FROM:
Pet, Cracked or Royal Egg
WANT
GOT
RARE

PET ADVENTURES, PART 3

The Red Panda and the Unicorn were still laughing from the Silly Duck's story as they continued on their way. They knew they had more puzzles to solve before they found the party!

Come on, Red Panda!

I need to rest for a moment. Shall we go to the Nursery to take a nap?

There's no time for naps – the treasure hunt hasn't finished yet!

You've solved two puzzles splendidly!

We hope that you don't tire.

The next one's at a place that has

Some tents by a campfire . . .

40

Ooh, I can guess where we're going next!

Me too! If we're right, I can take a nap there . . .

? Where should the Red Panda and the Unicorn head to? Circle the place you think they should visit, and then turn the page to see if you're correct!

HOSPITAL

SALON

CAMPSITE

At the Campsite, the Unicorn and the Red Panda searched the CAMPING SHOP and each tent carefully. Finally they saw it: PUZZLE #3 propped up on a log by the campfire!

PUZZLE #3

? Can you help solve the third clue?

Are you ready for s'more fun? In each group of sticks, cross out any with matching pairs. Then circle the one left over!

To spell out the third part of the secret message, write in the letters next to the marshmallow that didn't have a pair!

1

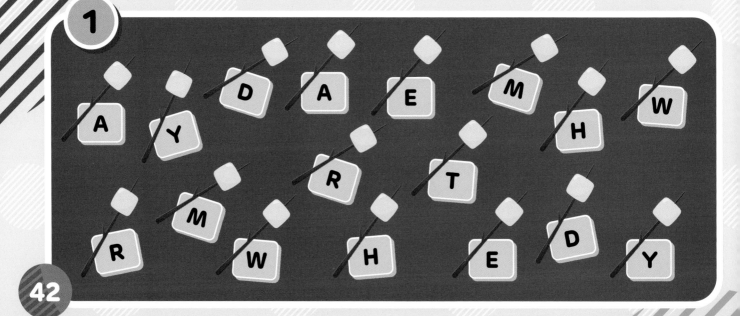

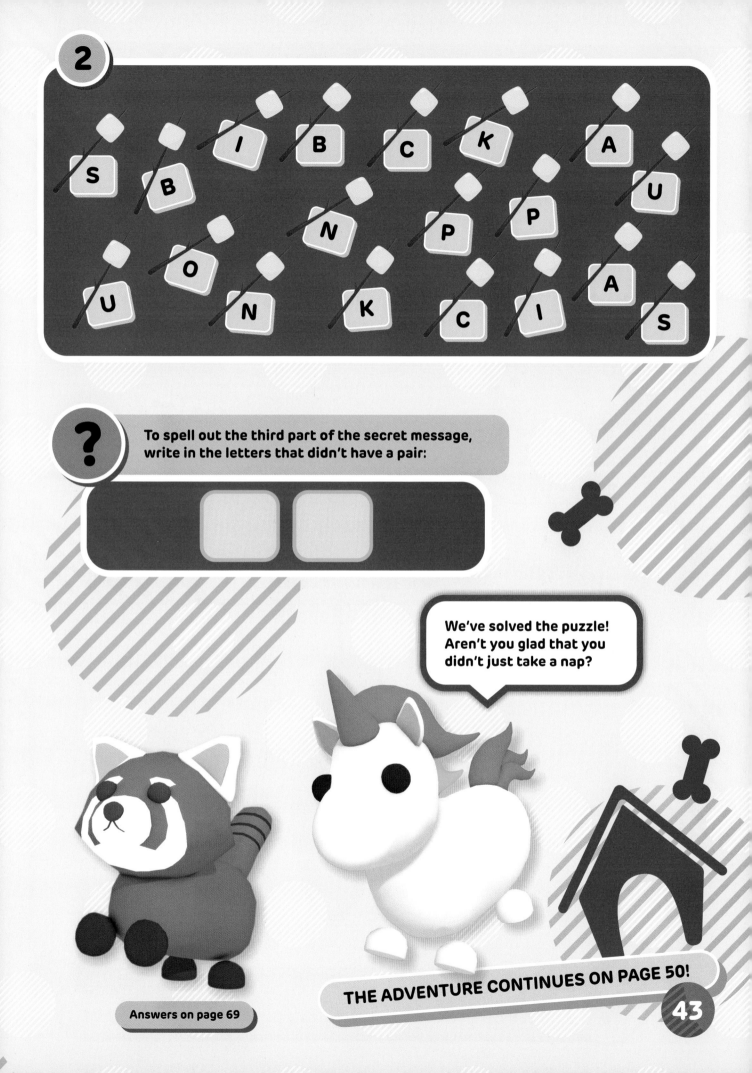

2

To spell out the third part of the secret message, write in the letters that didn't have a pair:

We've solved the puzzle! Aren't you glad that you didn't just take a nap?

THE ADVENTURE CONTINUES ON PAGE 50!

Answers on page 69

GUESS WHICH ACCESSORY!

Can you work out which of the accessories Bonny the shopkeeper is looking for? Read the clues below, and circle the right one!

1 The accessory is red.

2 The accessory is a hat.

3 The accessory looks like a type of food.

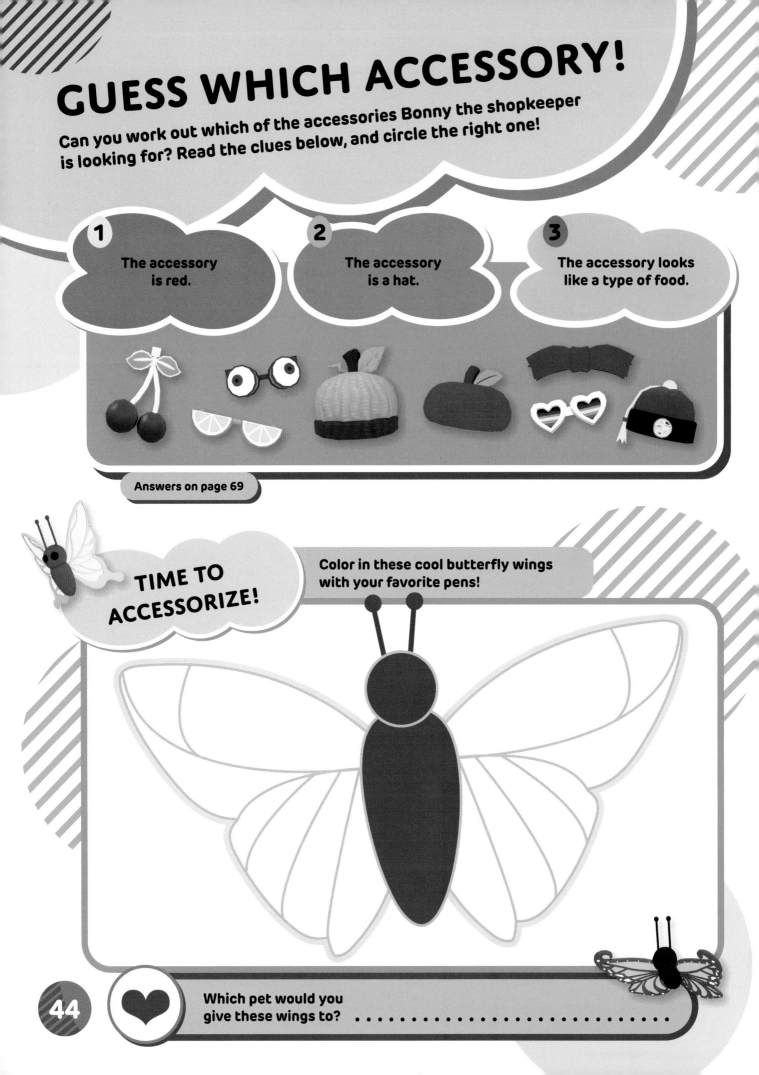

Answers on page 69

TIME TO ACCESSORIZE!

Color in these cool butterfly wings with your favorite pens!

Which pet would you give these wings to? . . . .

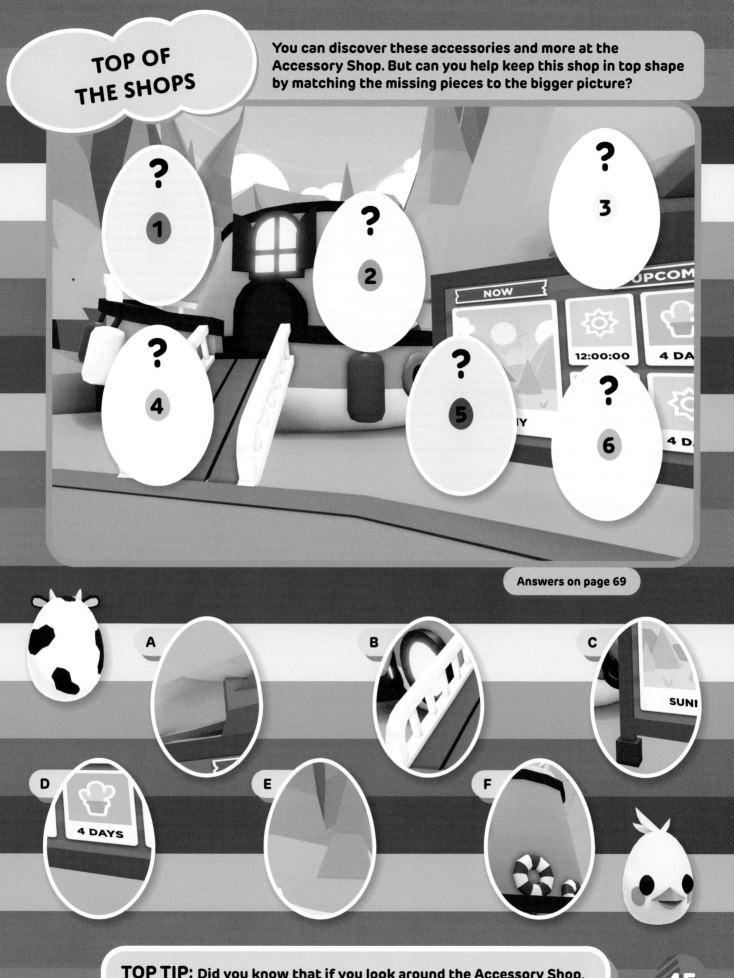

TOP OF THE SHOPS

You can discover these accessories and more at the Accessory Shop. But can you help keep this shop in top shape by matching the missing pieces to the bigger picture?

Answers on page 69

TOP TIP: Did you know that if you look around the Accessory Shop, you'll spot lots of pirate-themed decorations. Yarrr!

CRAFTING WITH CROW

There are so many accessories to choose from in the Accessory Shop. There are even free accessories: every hour, you can pick up a free badge for your pet.

Now here's a fun craft to do away from the computer – so you and your pet can match!

WHAT YOU'LL NEED:

I love *shiny* things! Here are my instructions for making a shiny badge to wear!

- A LARGE PIECE OF FELT
- A SAFETY PIN
- GLUE (WE RECOMMEND FABRIC GLUE OR HOT GLUE)
- THINGS TO DECORATE YOUR BADGE WITH, SUCH AS FELT SCRAPS, GLITTER OR BUTTONS
- A CUP TO TRACE AROUND
- SCISSORS
- A GROWN-UP TO HELP YOU!

STEP 1:

Trace a circle on a piece of felt. We've used a cup, but you can use the lid of a bottle, a jam jar lid or any circle! Repeat this step, so you have two circles of the same size. Cut both circles out carefully.

STEP 2:

Take one felt circle, and make two little openings to poke a safety pin through. This will be the bottom of your badge. Set this aside for now.

STEP 3:

Decorate your other circle with fabric scraps, glitter or buttons. This will be the top of your badge.

STEP 4:

Once the top circle has dried, glue its edges to the bottom circle. Line them up carefully, making sure the head of the safety pin is facing outwards.

STEP 5:

Carefully pin your badge on to your bag. Now you can match your pet!

TOP TIP: You could also pin it to your shirt or to a lanyard!

EVENT SPOTLIGHT:
HALLOWEEN EVENT

Halloween is the perfect time to gather your friends for some spectacularly spooky games!

HIDE-AND-SEEK

Can you find these nighttime animals hiding in the dark? Check them off when you spot them! But beware of the bats in the way!

TOP TIP: Some pets – like the bat – are only available during events. You can often buy these pets with candy, which you'll win from playing games. The more games you play, the more candy you'll collect!

Answers on page 69

SPOOKY SHADOWS

Can you match these pets to their shadows – and find one leftover shadow that doesn't belong to anyone?

1 2 3 4 5

A B C

D ? E F

? The extra shadow belongs to this pet: . . . .

TIGERS AND BEARS, OH MY!

Here's a Halloween riddle – but you can only solve it if you take away the tigers and bears (oh my!). Cross out the letters in the words TIGERS and BEARS below, then write out what's left!

RIDDLE: When do cows turn into werewolves?

ANSWER: During the:

TFIUGLELRS MBOEOOAROSOON

. . . .

Answers on page 69

PET ADVENTURES, PART 4

The Unicorn and the Red Panda kept searching all over Adoption Island! They ran past the ACCESSORY SHOP, the VEHICLE DEALERSHIP and the HOT SPRINGS. Wherever would they go next?

It feels like we've been going around in circles!

That's because it's a treasure hunt! We did know it was going to be tricky!

But where should we go NOW?

Let's work this out together . . .

The puzzles might get trickier,
You should get going soon!
To solve it, you must ride aboard
A swift Hot Air Balloon . . .

NOW

Do you know where we're going, Unicorn?

I do, and I know how to get there too.

? Where should the Unicorn and the Red Panda go? Circle the place you think the puzzle is hidden, and then turn the page to see if you're correct!

SUNNY

NEON CAVE

SKY CASTLE

SCHOOL

The moment that the Unicorn and the Red Panda boarded the Hot Air Balloon to take them to the SKY CASTLE, the hunt began! The final secret word was hidden along the flight . . .

PUZZLE #4

Can you help our friends by guiding them through the maze? Every time you pass a letter, write it below in pencil. You can always erase it if you make a mistake!

___ ___ ___

START

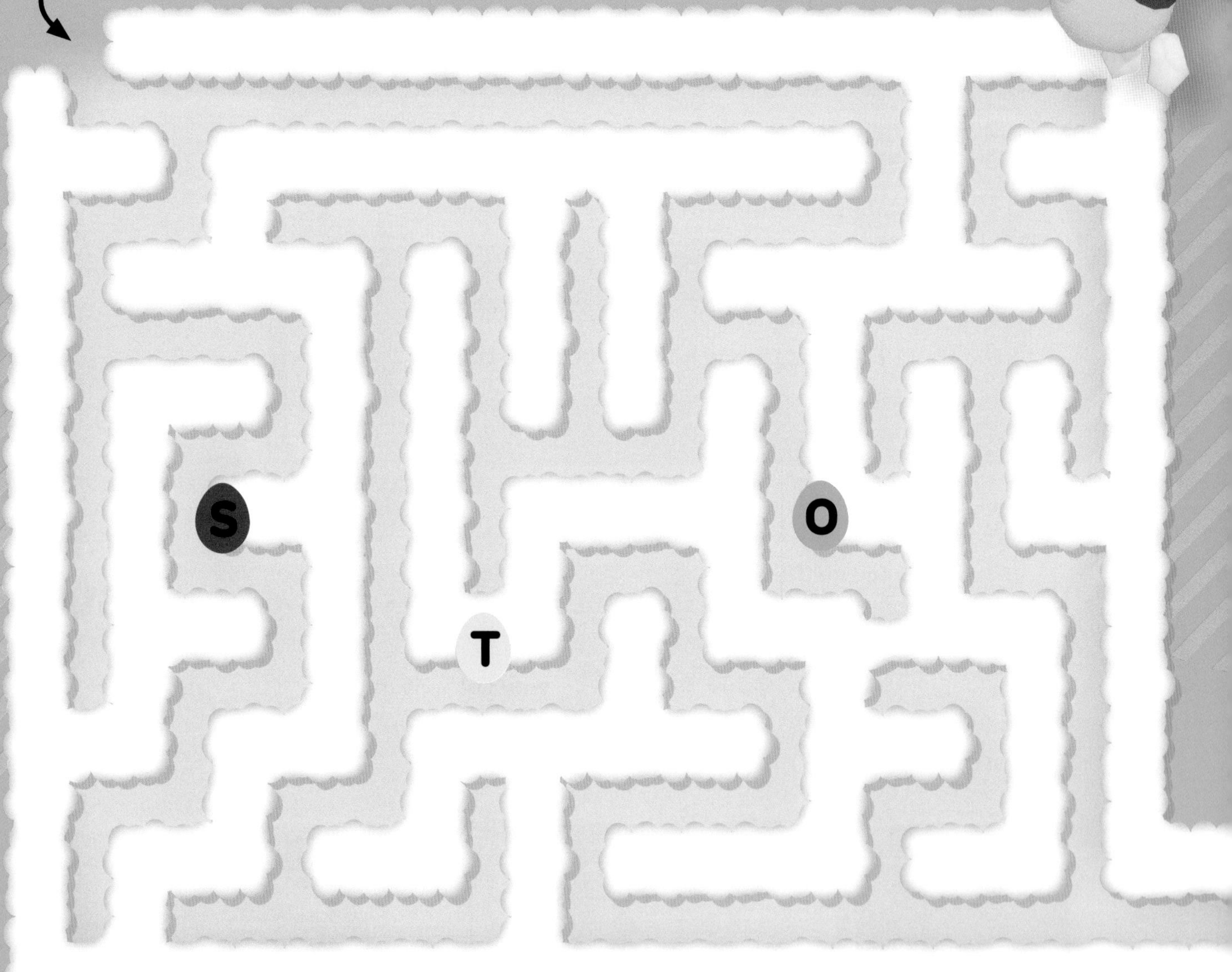

S

O

T

Answers on page 69

THE ADVENTURE CONTINUES ON PAGE 58!

SKY CASTLE ADVENTURES

The Red Panda and the Unicorn took their time exploring the Sky Castle, bouncing on the trampoline and looking down, down, down at **Adoption Island** below.

> Sometimes I wish that I could fly!

> Me too! But we were flying in the Hot Air Balloon.

> I wish I had my own Hot Air Balloon!

> What would your Hot Air Balloon look like?

> Well, I love to eat and I love to nap, so this is what it would be like . . .

? What sort of Hot Air Balloon is the Red Panda thinking of? You decide – and draw a picture of it below!

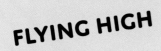

FLYING HIGH

The Red Panda wants a Hot Air Balloon, but there are many machines that let you fly. Now it's time to design your own. What colors will it be? How will it be powered? And what snacks will you have aboard? Draw it in the space below!

TOP TIP: You don't have to take the Hot Air Balloon to visit the Sky Castle – if you have a Glider, Propeller or a flyable pet, you can reach it that way!

POTION COMMOTION!

How well do you know your potions? Complete the names of these potions and match them to their descriptions below.

Anti-Gra __ __ ty

__ __ __ Head

Hyper__ __ __ ed

__ __ __ __ __ -A-Pet

Small __ __ __

Translucent __ __ __

A This potion, when fed to your pet, shrinks them for 10 minutes!

B This potion increases the size of your head!

C This potion lets you jump higher and higher!

D This potion makes you walk – or run – much faster!

E This potion, when fed to your pet, turns them translucent for ten minutes!

F This potion, when fed to your pet, makes them rideable forever!

TOP TIP: You can buy potions at the Sky Castle – and some can be brewed in a cauldron at your home!

Answers on page 69

ARE YOU A POTIONS MASTER?

Look at the list of potions below. Put a check in the "Real" box if you think it's a potion from Adopt Me, or put a check in the "Fake" box if you think it's made up!

			REAL	FAKE
1	**SNOWFLAKE POTION**	This potion creates a trail of snowflakes when you move!		
2	**PINK SHOES POTION**	This potion turns your shoes bright pink!		
3	**UNHATCHED POTION**	This potion turns your pet back into an egg!		
4	**HEART POTION**	This potion produces a heart effect around your body!		
5	**TELEPORTATION POTION**	This potion lets you teleport to your house or the Nursery.		

Answers on page 69

SOMETHING'S BREWING!

Time to invent a brand-new potion. Color in the bottle below with your brightest pens . . . and maybe add some magic sparkles!

When you drink my potion, this is what happens:

. . . .

. . . .

. . . .

PET ADVENTURES, PART 5

The Unicorn and the Red Panda had solved many puzzles together. But where could they find the party?

What's left?

There's just one more thing to read, and then we have to put everything together!

You've nearly solved the treasure hunt,
There's only one more part!
Go to the shop that's red and blue,
And there, the fun will start . . .

THE UNICORN AND THE RED PANDA LOOKED AT EACH OTHER ...

THE NURSERY!

THEY SHOUTED TOGETHER. AND OFF THEY DASHED.

WHEN THEY ARRIVED, THERE WAS A FINAL MESSAGE ON THE DOOR!

BUT WHAT DID IT MEAN?

I think we have to hold it up to a mirror.

PUZZLE #5

EGG SHOP

? Now can you help the Red Panda and the Unicorn find the party?
Go back through the Annual and put the clues together.

CLUE #1 | Page 17

CLUE #2 | Page 27

CLUE #3 | Page 43

CLUE #4 | Page 52

CLUE #5 | Page 59

59

Answers on page 69

Finally the Unicorn and the Red Panda had found the party! To celebrate, they were given a brand-new egg to design themselves. What should it look like? And what pets should hatch from it?

We did it! We solved all the puzzles!

And the new egg is so cute! But now it's YOUR TURN to color it in, and decide what pets it should hatch!

pet 1 _____

pet 2 _____

pet 3 _____

pet 4 _____

pet 5 _____

pet 6 _____

pet 7 _____

pet 8 _____

TOP TIPS – HOW TO DEVELOP YOUR OWN GAMES

Do you dream of making your own games one day? Here is some advice from the developers of Adopt Me!

SPEND LOTS OF TIME PLAYING AROUND AND TRYING NEW THINGS!

"My passion for game development began by playing other games, redesigning free models and then eventually making my own games. If you have a game development itch that needs a scratch, I highly recommend playing around with different games and seeing what you can create!" –Bethink

CREATE WHAT YOU WANT TO IMAGINE AND EXPLORE!

"As someone who played a lot of games as a kid, it was always a dream of mine to make my own game! I didn't like programming too much, so I focused on the art aspect more, messing around to make characters and worlds that I wanted to explore." –ColoredCookies

IT'S OK TO START SMALL!

"I started with simple 2D games and transitioned from engine to engine. Eventually, I found myself spending less of my time playing games and more of my time making them. The rest is history!" –EgoMoose

YOU CAN READ MORE ABOUT THE DEVELOPERS ON PAGE 12!

ADOPT ME QUIZ

Test your knowledge of the game with these questions!
How many can you get right?

Why not challenge a friend to take the quiz as well?

1 How do you travel between **the Neighborhood** and **Adoption Island?**

A **Take the Hot Air Balloon**

B **Go through the tunnel**

C **Open the door beneath the main bridge**

2 What are the basic starter pets?

A **Cats and Dogs**

B **Bats and Frogs**

C **Turkeys and Turtles**

3 What won't help you hatch an egg or age up your pet?

A **feeding it**

B **bathing it**

C **dressing it up**

4 Which of the following pets is Common?

A **Chicken**

B **Capybara**

C **Camel**

5 Which of the following pets is not Rare?

A **Unicorn**

B **Rhino**

C **Narwhal**

6 Which of the following pets is Legendary?

A **Wyvern**

B **Fallow Deer**

C **Pterodactyl**

7 How many Neon pets do you need to make a Mega Neon pet?

A **four**

B **five**

C **six**

8 How many different pets can be adopted?

A **over 100**

B **over 500**

C **over 1,000**

Answers on page 69

EVENT SPOTLIGHT:
WINTRY WONDERLAND!

Winter is the perfect time for skating across the ice and joining a snowball fight or two! Who knows – you may even adopt a new Ultra-Rare or Legendary pet!

Join in the festive fun with these winter games!

Make your way through the maze to the Ermine at the finish. How many gingerbread cookies can you collect along the way?

START

Answers on page 69

PENGUIN PAIRS

Can you match up six pairs of Penguins and find one left over?

BELIEVE IN YOUR ELF

You've acquired an Elf Hat, but it's just a bit too big for your pet! Can you figure out which pet is beneath each hat?

· ·

· ·

Answers on page 69

ANSWERS

Pages 10-11

ADOPTION ISLAND

1. The Nursery 2. The Hospital
3. The Playground 4. The Campsite
5. The Neon Cave

Pages 16-17

PET ADVENTURES, PART 1

P	L	D	E	A	R	F	R	I	T
E	I	E	N	E	D	S	P	S	O
P	S	A	U	S	A	G	E	N	M
P	A	T	H	E	E	F	P	O	A
E	B	I	R	E	S	T	P	I	T
R	W	O	R	H	D	Y	E	N	O
O	O	U	N	C	E	E	R	O	E
N	D	I	S	H	E	A	S	D	S
I	S	M	O	O	R	H	S	U	M

The leftover letters spell out: DEAR FRIENDS. THE FIRST WORD YOU NEED IS: "HEAD."

Pages 18-19

FEEDING FUN!

1. Ice Cream Cone 2. Popcorn
3. Raspberry Pie 4. Watermelon
5. Cheese 6. Hot Dog 7. Pizza

ODD DRINK OUT

Page 20

ROOM TO GROW

Page 22

PREPOSTEROUS PETS

Pudding Cat

Sprout Snail

Yule Log Dog

Pages 26-27

PET ADVENTURES, PART 2

Puffin: Orange, Polar Bear: Vanilla, Arctic Reindeer: Raspberry

Pages 30-31

CAR, PLANE OR TRAIN?

**1. Wing Trunk Car 2. Present Truck
3. Yellow Taxi Cab 4. Trireme
5. Tundra Exploration Machine
6. Dragon Train**

SPEEDY RACERS

1. B; 2. C; 3. A

Pages 42-43

PET ADVENTURES, PART 3

1. T; 2. O

Pages 44-45

GUESS WHICH ACCESSORY!

TOP OF THE SHOPS

1. E; 2. F; 3. A; 4. B; 5. C; 6. D

Pages 48-49

HIDE-AND-SEEK

SPOOKY SHADOWS

**1. C; 2. B; 3. E; 4. A; 5. F
Extra shadow D belongs to the Narwhal.**

TIGERS AND BEARS, OH MY!

FULL MOOOOOON

Pages 52-53

PET ADVENTURES, PART 4

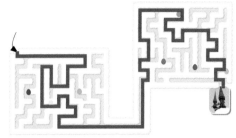

Pages 56-57

POTION COMMOTION!

**Anti-Gravity: C, Big Head: B,
Hyperspeed: D, Ride-A-Pet: F,
Small Sip: A, Translucent Tea: E**

ARE YOU A POTIONS MASTER?

**1. REAL 2. FAKE 3. FAKE 4. REAL
5. REAL**

Page 59

PET ADVENTURES, PART 5

HEAD OVER TO THE EGG SHOP.

Pages 64-65

ADOPT ME QUIZ

1. B; 2. A; 3. C; 4. A; 5. A; 6. B; 7. A; 8. A

Pages 66-67

WINTERY WONDERLAND!

PENGUIN PAIRS

The Penguin left over is:

BELIEVE IN YOUR ELF

**Ice Moth, Gingerbread Reindeer,
Snowball, Shortcake Dragon**